Favorite Picture Books
Illustrated by Gyo Fujikawa

Babies
Baby Animals
Come Follow Me
Oh, What a Busy Day!
Fairy Tales and Fables
The Night Before Christmas
Gyo Fujikawa's A to Z Picture Book
Gyo Fujikawa's Original Mother Goose
Gyo Fujikawa's Original
A Child's Garden of Verses

THIS BOOK BELONGS TO

Gyo Fujikawa's

A CHILD'S BOOK of POEMS

Publishers • **GROSSET & DUNLAP** • *New York*

A member of The Putnam Publishing Group
1989 Edition

Contents

WHICH IS THE WAY TO SOMEWHERE TOWN?

Which is the way to Somewhere Town?
    Oh, up in the morning early;
Over the tiles and the chimney pots,
    That is the way, quite clearly.

And which is the door to Somewhere Town?
    Oh, up in the morning early;
The round red sun is the door to go through,
    That is the way, quite clearly.

Kate Greenaway

SUMMER SUN

Great is the sun, and wide he goes
Through empty heaven without repose.
And in the blue and glowing days
More thick than rain he showers his rays.

Though closer still the blinds we pull
To keep the shady parlor cool,
Yet he will find a chink or two
To slip his golden fingers through.

The dusty attic spider-clad
He, through the keyhole, maketh glad;
And through the broken edge of tiles
Into the laddered hayloft smiles.

Meantime, his golden face around
He bares to all the garden ground,
And sheds a warm and glittering look
Among the ivy's inmost nook.

Above the hills, along the blue,
Round the bright air with footing true.
To please the child, to paint the rose,
The gardener of the world, he goes.

Robert Louis Stevenson

NIGHT

The sun descending in the west,
    The evening star does shine;
The birds are silent in their nest,
    And I must seek for mine.
The moon, like a flower,
In heaven's high bower,
With silent delight
Sits and smiles on the night.

Farewell, green fields and happy groves,
    Where flocks have took delight.
Where lambs have nibbled, silent moves
    The feet of angels bright;
Unseen they pour blessing,
And joy without ceasing,
On each bud and blossom,
And each sleeping bosom.

William Blake

WYNKEN, BLYNKEN, AND NOD

Wynken, Blynken, and Nod one night
   Sailed off in a wooden shoe —
Sailed on a river of crystal light,
   Into a sea of dew.
"Where are you going, and what do you wish?"
   The old moon asked the three.
"We have come to fish for the herring fish
   That live in this beautiful sea;
   Nets of silver and gold have we!"
       Said Wynken,
       Blynken,
       And Nod.

The old moon laughed and sang a song,
   As they rocked in the wooden shoe,
And the wind that sped them all night long
   Ruffled the waves of dew.
The little stars were the herring fish
   That lived in that beautiful sea —
"Now cast your nets wherever you wish —
   Never afeared are we";
   So cried the stars to the fishermen three:
       Wynken,
       Blynken,
       And Nod.

All night long their nets they threw
    To the stars in the twinkling foam —
Then down from the skies came the wooden shoe,
    Bringing the fishermen home;
'Twas all so pretty a sail it seemed
    As if it could not be,
And some folks thought 'twas a dream they'd dreamed
    Of sailing that beautiful sea —
    But I shall name you the fishermen three:
        Wynken,
        Blynken,
        And Nod.

Wynken and Blynken are two little eyes,
    And Nod is a little head,
And the wooden shoe that sailed the skies
    Is a wee one's trundle-bed.
So shut your eyes while mother sings
    Of wonderful sights that be,
And you shall see the beautiful things
    As you rock in the misty sea,
    Where the old shoe rocked the fishermen three:
        Wynken,
        Blynken,
        And Nod.

Eugene Field

HOW THEY SLEEP

Some things go to sleep in such a funny way:
Little birds stand on one leg and tuck their heads
    away;

Chickens do the same, standing on their perch;
Little mice lie soft and still, as if they were in
    church;

Kittens curl up close in such a funny ball;
Horses hang their sleepy heads and stand still in
    a stall;

Sometimes dogs stretch out, or curl up in a heap;
Cows lie down upon their sides when they would
    go to sleep.

But little babies dear are snugly tucked in beds,
Warm with blankets, all so soft, and pillows for
    their heads.

Bird and beast and babe — I wonder which of all
Dream the dearest dreams that down from
    dreamland fall!

FOUR DUCKS ON A POND

Four ducks on a pond,
A grass bank beyond,
A blue sky of spring,
White clouds on the wing;
What a little thing
To remember for years —
To remember with tears!

William Allingham

SUSAN BLUE

Oh, Susan Blue,
How do you do?
Please may I go for a walk with you?
Where shall we go?
Oh, I know —
Down in the meadow where the cowslips
    grow!

Kate Greenaway

CERTAINTY

I never saw a moor,
I never saw the sea;
Yet know I how the heather looks,
And what a wave must be.

I never spoke with God,
Nor visited in Heaven;
Yet certain am I of the spot
As if the chart were given.

Emily Dickinson

A CRADLE SONG

Golden slumbers kiss your eyes,
Smiles awake you when you rise.
Sleep, pretty wantons, do not cry,
And I will sing a lullaby:
Rock them, rock them, lullaby.

Care is heavy, therefore, sleep you;
You are care, and care must keep you.
Sleep, pretty wantons, do not cry,
And I will sing a lullaby:
Rock them, rock them, lullaby.

Thomas Dekker

OLD DOG

OLD DOG,
Why do you lie so still?
Are you thinking of when you were a pup?
Are you longing to be a pup?

OLD DOG,
Why do you lie so still?
Do you remember your mother?
Do you want your mother near you?

OLD DOG,
Why do you lie so still?
You must be dreaming of childhood.
You must be afraid to die.

OLD DOG,
Why do you lie so still?
Will you never wake up?
Won't you ever wake up?

Ann Covici

17

WHAT IS PINK? A ROSE IS PINK

What is pink? A rose is pink
    By the fountain's brink.
What is red? A poppy's red
    In its barley bed.
What is blue? The sky is blue
    Where the clouds float thro'.
What is white? A swan is white
    Sailing in the light.
What is yellow? A pear is yellow,
    Rich and ripe and mellow.
What is green? The grass is green
    With small flowers between.
What is violet? Clouds are violet
    In the summer twilight,
What is orange? Why, an orange,
    Just an orange!

Christina Rossetti

THE LITTLE ELFMAN

I met a little elfman once,
    Down where the lilies blow.
I asked him why he was so small,
    And why he didn't grow.

He slightly frowned, and with his eye
    He looked me through and through —
"I'm just as big for me," said he,
    "As you are big for you!"

John Kendrick Bangs

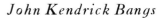

THE LILY PRINCESS

Down from her dainty head
The Lily Princess lightly drops
A spider's airy thread.

GOOD MORNING, MERRY SUNSHINE

Good morning, merry sunshine,
How did you wake so soon?
You've scared the little stars away,
And shined away the moon;
I saw you go to sleep last night,
Before I ceased my playing.
How did you get 'way over here,
And where have you been staying?

I never go to sleep, dear;
I just go round to see
My little children of the East
Who rise and watch for me.
I waken all the birds and bees,
And flowers on the way,
And last of all the little child
Who stayed out late to play.

THE CITY MOUSE AND THE
GARDEN MOUSE

The city mouse lives in a house;
    The garden mouse lives in a bower,
He's friendly with the frogs and toads,
    And sees the pretty plants in flower.

The city mouse eats bread and cheese;
    The garden mouse eats what he can;
We will not grudge him seeds and stocks,
    Poor little timid furry man.

Christina Rossetti

21

WHO HAS SEEN THE WIND?

Who has seen the wind?
 Neither I nor you;
But when the leaves hang trembling,
 The wind is passing through.

Who has seen the wind?
 Neither you nor I:
But when the trees bow down their heads,
 The wind is passing by.

      Christina Rossetti

THE FRIENDLY COW

The friendly cow, all red and white,
 I love with all my heart;
She gives me cream, with all her might,
 To eat with apple tart.

She wanders lowing here and there,
 And yet she cannot stray,
All in the pleasant open air,
 The pleasant light of day.

And blown by all the winds that pass
 And wet with all the showers,
She walks among the meadow grass
 And eats the meadow flowers.

    Robert Louis Stevenson

LITTLE WIND

Little wind, blow on the hilltop;
Little wind, blow on the plain,
Little wind, blow up the sunshine,
Little wind, blow off the rain.

Eenie, meenie, minie, mo,
Catch a tiger by the toe,
If he hollers, let him go,
Eenie, meenie, minie, mo.

Out goes the rat,
Out goes the cat,
Out goes the lady
With the big green hat.
Y, O, U, spells you;
O, U, T, spells out!

One potato, two potato,
Three potato, four;
Five potato, six potato,
Seven potato, MORE.

One-ery, Two-ery, Ickery, Ann,
Phillip-son, Phollop-son, Nicholas, John,
    Queevy, Quavy,
    English Navy,
Zinglum, Zanglum, Bolun, Bun.

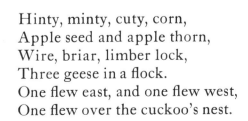

Hinty, minty, cuty, corn,
Apple seed and apple thorn,
Wire, briar, limber lock,
Three geese in a flock.
One flew east, and one flew west,
One flew over the cuckoo's nest.

THE NAUGHTY BOY

There was a naughty boy,
  And a naughty boy was he,
He ran away to Scotland
  The people for to see —
    Then he found
    That the ground
    Was as hard,
    That a yard
    Was as long,
    That a song
    Was as merry,
    That a cherry
    Was as red,
    That lead
    Was as weighty,
    That fourscore
    Was as eighty,
    That a door
    Was as wooden
    As in England —
So he stood in his shoes
  And he wondered,
  He wondered.
He stood in his shoes
  And he wondered.

John Keats

TO AN INSECT

Thou art a female, katydid!
  I know it by the trill
That quivers through thy piercing notes,
  So petulant and shrill;
I think there is a knot of you
  Beneath the hollow tree —
A knot of spinster katydids —
  Do katydids drink tea?

Oliver Wendell Holmes

FERRY ME ACROSS
THE WATER

"Ferry me across the water,
  Do, boatman, do."
"If you've a penny in your purse,
  I'll ferry you."

"I have a penny in my purse,
  And my eyes are blue;
So ferry me across the water,
  Do, boatman, do!"

"Step into my ferryboat,
  Be they black or blue,
And for the penny in your purse
  I'll ferry you."

Christina Rossetti

THE OWL AND THE PUSSYCAT

The Owl and the Pussycat went to sea
    In a beautiful pea-green boat;
They took some honey, and plenty of money
    Wrapped up in a five-pound note.
The Owl looked up to the stars above,
    And sang to a small guitar,
"O lovely Pussy, O Pussy, my love,
    What a beautiful Pussy you are,
      You are,
      You are!
    What a beautiful Pussy you are!"

Pussy said to the Owl, "You elegant fowl,
    How charmingly sweet you sing!
Oh! let us be married; too long we have
      tarried:
    But what shall we do for a ring?"
They sailed away, for a year and a day,
    To the land where the bong-tree grows,
And there in a wood a Piggy-wig stood,
    With a ring at the end of his nose,
      His nose,
      His nose,
    With a ring at the end of his nose.

"Dear Pig, are you willing to sell for one
      shilling
    Your ring?" Said the Piggy, "I will."
So they took it away, and were married next
      day
    By the turkey who lives on the hill.
They dined on mince and slices of quince,
    Which they ate with a runcible spoon;
And hand in hand, on the edge of the sand,
    They danced by the light of the moon,
      The moon,
      The moon,
    They danced by the light of the moon.

Edward Lear

THE OWL

When cats run home and light is come,
And dew is cold upon the ground,
And the far-off stream is dumb,
And the whirring sail goes round;
Alone and warming his five wits,
The white owl in the belfry sits.

When merry milkmaids click the latch,
And rarely smells the new-mown hay,
And the cock hath sung beneath the thatch
Twice or thrice his roundelay;
Alone and warming his five wits,
The white owl in the belfry sits.

Alfred, Lord Tennyson

THE HUMMINGBIRD

The hummingbird, the hummingbird,
So fairy-like and bright;
It lives among the sunny flowers,
A creature of delight.

Mary Howitt

THE OSTRICH IS A SILLY BIRD

The ostrich is a silly bird
With scarcely any mind.
He often runs so very fast,
He leaves himself behind.

And when he gets there, has to stand
And hang about till night,
Without a blessed thing to do
Until he comes in sight.

Mary E. Wilkins Freeman

28

THE FLEA AND THE FLY

A flea and a fly got caught in a flue.
   Said the fly, "Let us flee."
   Said the flea, "Let us fly."
So together they flew through a flaw in the flue.

PEAS

I eat my peas with honey,
I've done it all my life,
They do taste kind of funny,
But it keeps them on the knife.

MR. NOBODY

I know a funny little man,
   As quiet as a mouse,
Who does the mischief that is done
   In everybody's house!
There's no one ever sees his face,
   And yet we all agree
That every plate we break was cracked
   By Mr. Nobody.

'Tis he who always tears our books,
   Who leaves the door ajar,
He pulls the buttons from our shirts,
   And scatters pins afar;
That squeaking door will always squeak,
   For, prithee, don't you see,
We leave the oiling to be done
   By Mr. Nobody.

The fingermarks upon the door
   By none of us are made;
We never leave the blinds unclosed,
   To let the curtains fade.
The ink we never spill; the boots
   That lying round you see
Are not our boots — they all belong
   To Mr. Nobody.

THE DUEL

The gingham dog and the calico cat
Side by side on the table sat;
'Twas half-past twelve, and (what do you think!)
Nor one nor t' other had slept a wink!
  The old Dutch clock and the Chinese plate
  Appeared to know as sure as fate
There was going to be a terrible spat.
  (I wasn't there; I simply state
  What was told to me by the Chinese plate!)

The gingham dog went, "Bow-wow-wow!"
And the calico cat replied, "Mee-ow!"
The air was littered, an hour or so,
With bits of gingham and calico,
  While the old Dutch clock in the chimney-place
  Up with its hands before its face,
For it always dreaded a family row!
  (Now mind: I'm only telling you
  What the old Dutch clock declares is true!)

The Chinese plate looked very blue,
And wailed, "Oh, dear! what shall we do!"
But the gingham dog and the calico cat
Wallowed this way and tumbled that,
  Employing every tooth and claw
  In the awfullest way you ever saw —
And, oh! how the gingham and calico flew!
  (Don't fancy I exaggerate —
  I got my news from the Chinese plate!)

Next morning, where the two had sat
They found no trace of dog or cat;
And some folks think unto this day
That burglars stole that pair away!
  But the truth about the cat and pup
  Is this: they ate each other up!
Now what do you really think of that!
  (The old Dutch clock it told me so,
  And that is how I came to know.)

Eugene Field

THE MILK JUG

(The Kitten Speaks)

The Gentle Milk Jug blue and white
    I love with all my soul;
She pours herself with all her might
    To fill my breakfast bowl.

All day she sits upon the shelf,
    She does not jump or climb —
She only waits to pour herself
    When 'tis my suppertime.

And when the Jug is empty quite,
    I shall not mew in vain,
The Friendly Cow all red and white,
    Will fill her up again.

Oliver Herford

CHOOSING A KITTEN

A black-nosed kitten will slumber all the day;
A white-nosed kitten is ever glad to play;
A yellow-nosed kitten will answer to your call;
And a gray-nosed kitten I like best of all.

I HAD A LITTLE DOGGY

I had a little Doggy that used to sit and beg;
But Doggy tumbled down the stairs and broke his little leg.
Oh! Doggy, I will nurse you, and try to make you well,
And you shall have a collar with a little silver bell.

Ah! Doggy, don't you think that you should very faithful be,
For having such a loving friend to comfort you as me?
And when your leg is better, and you can run and play,
We'll have a scamper in the fields and see them making hay.

But, Doggy, you must promise (and mind your word to keep)
Not once to tease the little lambs, or run among the sheep;
And then the little yellow chicks that play upon the grass,
You must not even wag your tail to scare them as you pass.

NESTING TIME

Wrens and robins in the hedge,
  Wrens and robins here and there;
Building, perching, pecking, fluttering,
  Everywhere!

Christina Rossetti

HURT NO LIVING THING

Hurt no living thing:
  Ladybird, nor butterfly,
Nor moth with dusty wing,
  Nor cricket chirping cheerily,
Nor grasshopper so light of leap,
  Nor dancing gnat, nor beetle fat,
Nor harmless worms that creep.

Christina Rossetti

THE CALL

Come, calf, now to mother,
Come, lamb, that I choose,
Come, cats, one and t'other,
With snowy-white shoes,
Come, gosling all yellow,
Come forth with your fellow,
Come, chickens so small,
Scarce walking at all,
Come, doves, that are mine now,
With feathers so fine now!
The grass is bedewed,
The sunlight renewed,
It's early, early, summer's advancing
But autumn soon comes a-dancing!

Bjornsterne Bjornson

BE LIKE THE BIRD

Be like the bird, who
Halting in his flight
On limb too slight
Feels it give way beneath him,
Yet sings,
Knowing he hath wings.

Victor Hugo

IN A CHILD'S ALBUM

Small service is true service while it lasts;
Of humblest friends, bright creature, scorn not one;
The daisy, by the shadow that it casts,
Protects the lingering dewdrop from the sun.

William Wordsworth

KINDNESS TO ANIMALS

Little children, never give
Pain to things that feel and live;
Let the gentle robin come
For the crumbs you save at home;
As his meat you throw along
He'll repay you with a song.
Never hurt the timid hare
Peeping from her green grass lair,
Let her come and sport and play
On the lawn at close of day.
The little lark goes soaring high
To the bright windows of the sky,
Singing as if 'twere always spring,
And fluttering on an untired wing —
Oh! let him sing his happy song,
Nor do these gentle creatures wrong.

THANKSGIVING DAY

Over the river and through the wood,
   To Grandfather's house we go;
     The horse knows the way
     To carry the sleigh
   Through the white and drifted snow.

Over the river and through the wood —
   Oh, how the wind does blow!
     It stings the toes
     And bites the nose
   As over the ground we go.

Over the river and through the wood,
   To have a first-rate play.
     Hear the bells ring,
     "Ting-a-ling-ding!"
   Hurrah for Thanksgiving Day!

Over the river and through the wood,
   Trot fast, my dapple-gray!
     Spring over the ground
     Like a hunting hound,
   For this is Thanksgiving Day

Over the river and through the wood,
   And straight through the barnyard gate.
     We seem to go
     Extremely slow —
   It is so hard to wait!

Over the river and through the wood —
   Now Grandmother's cap I spy!
     Hurrah for the fun!
     Is the pudding done?
   Hurrah for the pumpkin pie!

Lydia Maria Child

TURKEY TIME

Thanksgiving Day will soon be here;
It comes around but once a year.
If I could only have my way,
We'd have Thanksgiving every day!

NOVEMBER

I love the fitful gust that shakes
   The casement all the day,
And from the glossy elm tree takes
   The faded leaves away,
Twirling them by the windowpane
With thousands others down the lane.

I love to see the cottage smoke
   Curl upward through the trees,
The pigeons nestled round the cote,
   November days like these;
The cock upon the woodland crowing,
The mill sails on the heath a-going.

John Clare

SING A SONG OF SEASONS

Sing a song of seasons!
   Something bright in all!
Flowers in the summer,
   Fires in the fall!

Robert Louis Stevenson

AUTUMN

The morns are meeker than they were,
   The nuts are getting brown;
The berry's cheek is plumper,
   The rose is out of town.

The maple wears a gayer scarf,
   The field a scarlet gown.
Lest I should be old-fashioned,
   I'll put a trinket on.

Emily Dickinson

MERRY AUTUMN DAYS

'Tis pleasant on a fine spring morn
    To see the buds expand,
'Tis pleasant in the summertime
    To see the fruitful land;
'Tis pleasant on a winter's night
    To sit around the blaze,
But what are joys like these, my boys,
    To merry autumn days!

We hail the merry autumn days,
    When leaves are turning red;
Because they're far more beautiful
    Than anyone has said.
We hail the merry harvest time,
    The gayest of the year;
The time of rich and bounteous crops,
    Rejoicing and good cheer.

Charles Dickens

THE FROST SPIRIT

He comes, he comes, the Frost Spirit comes! You may trace his footsteps now
On the naked woods and the blasted fields and the brown hill's withered brow.
He has smitten the leaves of the gray old trees where their pleasant green came forth,
And the winds, which follow wherever he goes, have shaken them down to earth.

John Greenleaf Whittier

WINTER

Bread and milk for breakfast,
   And woolen frocks to wear,
And a crumb for robin redbreast
   On the cold days of the year.

Christina Rossetti

CHRISTMAS BELLS

I heard the bells on Christmas Day
Their old, familiar carols play,
    And wild and sweet
    The words repeat
Of peace on earth, good will to men!

And thought how, as the day had come,
The belfries of all Christendom
    Had rolled along
    The unbroken song
Of peace on earth, good will to men!

Till, ringing, singing, on its way,
The world revolved from night to day,
    A voice, a chime,
    A chant sublime
Of peace on earth, good will to men!

Henry Wadsworth Longfellow

SANTA CLAUS AND THE MOUSE

One Christmas, when Santa Claus
    Came to a certain house,
To fill the children's stockings there,
    He found a little mouse.

"A Merry Christmas, little friend,"
    Said Santa good and kind.
"The same to you, sir," said the mouse,
    "I thought you wouldn't mind,

If I should stay awake tonight
    And watch you for a while."
"You're very welcome, little mouse,"
    Said Santa, with a smile.

And then he filled the stockings up
    Before the mouse could wink —
From toe to top, from top to toe,
    There wasn't left a chink.

"Now they won't hold another thing,"
    Said Santa Claus with pride.
A twinkle came in mouse's eyes,
    But humbly he replied:

"It's not polite to contradict —
    Your pardon I implore —
But in the fullest stocking there
    I could put one thing more."

"Oh, ho!" laughed Santa. "Silly mouse,
   Don't I know how to pack?
By filling stockings all these years
   I should have learned the knack."

And then he took the stocking down
   From where it hung so high,
And said, "Now put in one thing more,
   I give you leave to try."

The mousie chuckled to himself,
   And then he softly stole
Right to the stocking's crowded toe
   And gnawed a little hole!

"Now, if you please, good Santa Claus,
   I've put in one thing more,
For you will own that little hole
   Was not in there before."

How Santa Claus did laugh and laugh!
   And then he gaily spoke,
"Well, you shall have a Christmas cheese
   For that nice little joke!"

If you don't think this story is true,
   Why, I can show to you
The very stocking with the hole
   The little mouse gnawed through!

Emilie Poulsson

THE MONTHS

January brings the snow,
Makes our feet and fingers glow.

February brings the rain,
Thaws the frozen lake again.

May brings flocks of pretty lambs,
Skipping by their fleecy dams.

June brings tulips, lilies, roses,
Fills the children's hands with posies.

Warm September brings the fruit;
Sportsmen then begin to shoot.

Fresh October brings the pheasant;
Then to gather nuts is pleasant.

March brings breezes loud and shrill,
Stirs the dancing daffodil.

April brings the primrose sweet,
Scatters daisies at our feet.

Hot July brings cooling showers,
Apricots and gillyflowers.

August brings the sheaves of corn;
Then the harvest home is borne.

Dull November brings the blast,
When the leaves are whirling fast.

Chill December brings the sleet,
Blazing fires and Christmas treat.

Sara Coleridge

TONY O

Over the bleak and barren snow
A voice there came a-calling;
"Where are you going to, Tony O!
Where are you going this morning?"

"I am going where there are rivers of wine,
The mountains bread and honey:
There Kings and Queens do mind the swine,
And the poor have all the money."

Colin Francis

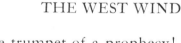

DOLL'S WALK

I took my dolly for a walk.
Before we reached the gate,
She kicked her little slipper off,
And soon she lost the mate.

THE WEST WIND

The trumpet of a prophecy! O Wind,
If winter comes, can spring be far behind?

Percy Bysshe Shelley

THE SNOWMAN

Once there was a snowman
    Stood outside the door
Thought he'd like to come inside
    And run around the floor;
Thought he'd like to warm himself
    By the firelight red;
Thought he'd like to climb up
    On that big white bed.
So he called the North Wind, "Help me now, I pray.
    I'm completely frozen, standing here all day."
So the North Wind came along and blew him in the door,
    And now there's nothing left of him
But a puddle on the floor!

44

INSCRIBED ON THE COLLAR OF A DOG

I am his Highness' dog at Kew;
Pray tell me, sir — whose dog are you?

Alexander Pope

OLD SONG

Haste thee, Winter, haste away!
Far too long has been thy stay.

English Couplet

ONE STORMY NIGHT

Two little kittens,
   One stormy night,
Began to quarrel,
   And then to fight.

One had a mouse,
   The other had none;
And that's the way
   The quarrel begun.

"I'LL have that mouse,"
   Said the bigger cat.
"YOU'LL have that mouse?
   We'll see about that!"

"I WILL have that mouse,"
   Said the eldest son.
"You SHA'NT have the mouse,"
   Said the little one.

The old woman seized
   Her sweeping broom,
And swept both kittens
   Right out of the room.

The ground was covered
   With frost and snow,
And the two little kittens
   Had nowhere to go.

They lay and shivered
   On a mat at the door
While the old woman
   Was sweeping the floor.

And then they crept in,
   As quiet as mice,
All wet with the snow,
   And as cold as ice,

And found it much better,
   That stormy night,
To lie by the fire
   Than to quarrel and fight.

Traditional

THE CROCODILE

How doth the little crocodile
    Improve his shining tail,
And pour the waters of the Nile
    On every golden scale!

How cheerfully he seems to grin,
    How neatly spreads his claws,
And welcomes little fishes in,
    With gently smiling jaws!

Lewis Carroll

WHEN YOU AND I GROW UP

When you and I
Grow up — Polly —
    I mean that you and me
Shall go sailing in a big ship
    Right over all the sea.
We'll wait till we are older,
    For if we went today,
You know that we might lose ourselves,
    And never find the way.

Kate Greenaway

THE GOLDEN RULE

To do to others as I would
    That they should do to me,
Will make me gentle, kind and good,
    As children ought to be.

TWENTY FROGGIES

Twenty froggies went to school
Down beside a rushy pool.
Twenty little coats of green,
Twenty vests all white and clean.

"We must be in time," said they,
"First we study, then we play;
That is how we keep the rule,
When we froggies go to school."

Master Bullfrog, brave and stern,
Called his classes in their turn,
Taught them how to nobly strive,
Also how to leap and dive;

Taught them how to dodge a blow,
From the sticks that bad boys throw.
Twenty froggies grew up fast,
Bullfrogs they became at last;

Polished in a high degree,
As each froggie ought to be,
Now they sit on other logs,
Teaching other little frogs.

George Cooper

WINGS

Oh that I had wings like a dove!
For then would I fly away and be at rest.
Lo, then would I wander far off,
And remain in the wilderness.

A Psalm of David

GOOD NIGHT

Baby, baby, lay your head
On your pretty cradle bed ;
Shut your eye-peeps, now the day
And the light are gone away ;
All the clothes are tuck'd in tight ;
Little baby, dear, good night.

Yes, my darling, well I know
How the bitter wind doth blow ;
And the winter's snow and rain
Patter on the windowpane ;
But they cannot come in here,
To my little baby dear.

For the window shutteth fast,
Till the stormy night is past,
And the curtains warm are spread
Roundabout her cradle bed ;
So till morning shineth bright,
Little baby, dear, good night.

Jane Taylor

FROM THE BRIDGE

How silent comes the water round that bend !
Not the minutest whisper does it send
To the o'erhanging willows : blades of grass
Slowly across the checkered shadows pass.

John Keats

THE FUNNY OLD MAN AND HIS WIFE

Once upon a time, in a little wee house,
   Lived a funny old man and his wife ;
And he said something funny to make her laugh,
   Every day of his life.

One day he said such a very funny thing,
   That she shook and screamed with laughter ;
But the poor old soul, she couldn't leave off
   For at least three whole days after.

So laughing with all her might and main,
   Three days and nights she sat ;
And at the end she didn't know a bit
   What she'd been laughing at.

THE FAIRIES

Up the airy mountain,
    Down the rushy glen,
We daren't go a-hunting,
    For fear of little men.
Wee folk, good folk,
    Trooping all together;
Green jacket, red cap,
    And white owl's feather!

Down along the rocky shore
    Some make their home.
They live on crispy pancakes
    Of yellow tide-foam;
Some in the reeds
    Of the black mountain lake,
With frogs for their watchdogs,
    All night awake.

William Allingham

THE VIOLET

A violet by a mossy stone,
Half hidden from the eye,
Fair as a star, when only one
Is shining in the sky.

William Wordsworth

MY FAIRY

I'd like to tame a fairy,
  To keep it on a shelf,
To see it wash its little face,
  And dress its little self.
I'd teach it pretty manners,
  It always should say "Please,"
And then, you know, I'd make it sew,
  And curtsy with its knees!

EXTREMES

A little boy once played so loud
That the thunder, up in a thundercloud,
Said, "Since *I* can't be heard, why, then,
I'll never, never thunder again!"

And a little girl once kept so still
That she heard a fly on the window sill
Whisper and say to a ladybird,
"She's the stillest child I ever heard!"

James Whitcomb Riley

DON'T GIVE UP

If you've tried and have not won,
  Never stop for crying;
All that's great and good is done
  Just by patient trying.

If by easy work you beat,
  Who the more will prize you?
Gaining victory from defeat,
  That's the test that tries you.

Phoebe Cary

THE PANCAKE

Mix a pancake,
Stir a pancake,
  Pop it in the pan;
Fry the pancake,
Toss the pancake —
  Catch it if you can!

Christina Rossetti

SONG

Tomorrow is Saint Valentine's day,
    All in the morning betime,
And I a maid at your window,
    To be your Valentine.

William Shakespeare

THE LITTLE PEACH

A little peach in the orchard grew —
A little peach of emerald hue;
Warmed by the sun and wet by the dew,
        It grew.

One day, passing the orchard through,
That little peach dawned on the view
Of Johnnie Jones and his sister Sue —
        Those two.

Up at the peach a club he threw —
Down from the tree on which it grew
Fell the little peach of emerald hue —
        Mon dieu!

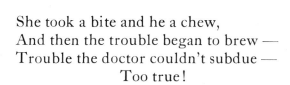

She took a bite and he a chew,
And then the trouble began to brew —
Trouble the doctor couldn't subdue —
        Too true!

Under the turf where the daisies grew
They planted John and his sister Sue,
And their little souls to the angels flew —
        Boo-hoo!

But what of the peach of emerald hue,
Warmed by the sun and wet by the dew?
Ah, well, its mission on earth was through —
        Adieu!

Eugene Field

LO, THE WINTER IS PAST

For, lo, the winter is past,
The rain is over and gone;
The flowers appear on the earth;
The time of the singing of birds is come,
And the voice of the turtle is heard in our land.

The Song of Solomon

PIPPA'S SONG

The year's at the spring
And the day's at the morn;
Morning's at seven;
The hillside's dew-pearled;
The lark's on the wing;
The snail's on the thorn:
God's in his heaven —
All's right with the world!

Robert Browning

SPRING

Sound the flute!
Now it's mute.
Birds delight
Day and night;
Nightingale
In the dale,
Lark in sky,
Merrily,
Merrily, merrily, to welcome in the year.

Little boy,
Full of joy;
Little girl,
Sweet and small;
Cock does crow,
So do you;
Merry voice,
Infant noise,
Merrily, merrily, to welcome in the year.

Little lamb
Here I am;
Come and lick
My white neck;
Let me pull
Your soft wool;
Let me kiss
Your soft face;
Merrily, merrily, we welcome in the year.

William Blake

MR. FINNEY'S TURNIP

Mr. Finney had a turnip
    And it grew behind the barn;
And it grew and it grew,
    And that turnip did no harm.

There it grew and it grew
    Till it could grow no longer;
Then his daughter Lizzie picked it
    And put it in the cellar.

There it lay and it lay
    Till it began to rot;
And his daughter Susie took it
    And put it in the pot.

And they boiled it and boiled it
    As long as they were able;
And then his daughters took it
    And put it on the table.

Mr. Finney and his wife
    They sat them down to sup;
And they ate and they ate
    And they ate that turnip up.

A SNACK

Three plum buns
    To eat here at the stile
In the clover meadow,
    For we have walked a mile.

One for you, and one for me,
    And one left over.
Give it to the boy who shouts
    To scare sheep from the clover.

Christina Rossetti

56

THE OLD MAN WITH A BEARD

There was an old man with a beard
Who said, "It is just as I feared!
    Two owls and a hen,
    Four larks and a wren,
Have all built their nests in my beard!"

Edward Lear

TWO IN BED

When my brother Tommy
    Sleeps in bed with me,
        He doubles up
        And makes
            himself
            exactly
            like
            a
            V

ALGY MET A BEAR

Algy met a bear,
The bear was bulgy,
The bulge was Algy.

And 'cause the bed is not so wide,
A part of him is on my side.

A. B. Ross

57

QUEEN MAB

A little fairy comes at night,
Her eyes are blue, her hair is brown,
With silver spots upon her wings,
And from the moon she flutters down.

She has a little silver wand,
And when a good child goes to bed
She waves her hand from right to left,
And makes a circle round its head.

And then it dreams of pleasant things,
Of fountains filled with fairy fish,
And trees that bear delicious fruit,
And bow their branches at a wish:

Of arbors filled with dainty scents
From lovely flowers that never fade;
Bright flies that glitter in the sun,
And glowworms shining in the shade:

And talking birds with gifted tongues,
For singing songs and telling tales,
And pretty dwarfs to show the way
Through fairy hills and fairy dales.

Thomas Hood

THE DAY IS DONE

The day is done, and the darkness
　Falls from the wings of Night,
As a feather is wafted downward
　From an eagle in his flight.

I see the lights of the village
　Gleam through the rain and the mist,
And a feeling of sadness comes o'er me
　That my soul cannot resist:

A feeling of sadness and longing,
　That is not akin to pain,
And resembles sorrow only
　As the mist resembles the rain.

Come, read to me some poem,
　Some simple and heartfelt lay,
That shall soothe this restless feeling,
　And banish the thoughts of day.

Not from the grand old masters,
　Not from the bards sublime,
Whose distant footsteps echo
　Through the corridors of Time.

For, like strains of martial music,
　Their mighty thoughts suggest
Life's endless toil and endeavor;
　And tonight I long for rest.

Read from some humbler poet,
　Whose songs gushed from his heart,
As showers from the clouds of summer,
　Or tears from the eyelids start;

Who, through long days of labor,
　And nights devoid of ease,
Still heard in his soul the music
　Of wonderful melodies.

Such songs have power to quiet
　The restless pulse of care,
And come like a benediction
　That follows after prayer.

Then read from the treasured volume
　The poem of thy choice,
And lend to the rhyme of the poet
　The beauty of thy voice.

And the night shall be filled with music,
　And the cares that infest the day,
Shall fold their tents, like the Arabs,
　And as silently steal away.

Henry Wadsworth Longfellow

SCHOOL IS OVER

School is over,
  Oh, what fun!
Lessons finished,
  Play begun.
Who'll run fastest,
  You or I?
Who'll laugh loudest?
  Let us try.

Kate Greenaway

A WEDDING

Rosy apple, lemon and pear,
  Bunch of roses she shall wear,
Gold and silver by her side,
  I know who shall be my bride.

London Street Game

LET DOGS DELIGHT

Let dogs delight to bark and bite,
For God hath made them so.

Isaac Watts

ALL THE BELLS WERE RINGING

All the bells were ringing
And all the birds were singing,
When Molly sat down crying
  For her broken doll:
  O you silly Moll!
Sobbing and sighing
  For a broken doll,
When all the bells are ringing,
And all the birds are singing.

Christina Rossetti

THE ECHOING GREEN

The sun does arise,
And make happy the skies;
The merry bells ring
To welcome the spring;
The skylark and thrush,
The birds of the bush,
Sing louder around
To the bell's cheerful sound,
While our sports shall be seen
On the echoing green.

Old John with white hair
Does laugh away care,
Sitting under the oak
Among the old folk.
They laugh at our play,
And soon they all say:
"Such, such were the joys
When we, all girls and boys,
In our youth-time were seen
On the echoing green."

Till the little ones, weary,
No more can be merry;
The sun does descend,
And our sports have an end.
Round the laps of their mothers,
Many sisters and brothers,
Like birds in their nest,
Are ready for rest;
And sport no more seen
On the echoing green.

William Blake

THE GRASSHOPPER
AND THE ELEPHANT

Way down south where bananas grow,
A grasshopper stepped on an elephant's
toe.
The elephant said, with tears in his eyes,
"Pick on somebody your own size."

RAIN IN SUMMER

How beautiful is the rain!
After the dust and heat,
In the broad and fiery street,
In the narrow lane,
How beautiful is the rain!
How it clatters along the roofs,
Like the tramp of hoofs!

How it gushes and struggles out
From the throat of the overflowing spout!
Across the windowpane
It pours and pours;
And swift and wide,
With a muddy tide,
Like a river down the gutter roars
The rain, the welcome rain!

Henry Wadsworth Longfellow

WHO IS TAPPING AT MY WINDOW?

"It's not I," said the cat.
"It's not I," said the rat.

"It's not I," said the wren.
"It's not I," said the hen.

"It's not I," said the fox.
"It's not I," said the ox.

"It's not I," said the loon.
"It's not I," said the coon.

"It's not I," said the cony.
"It's not I," said the pony.

"It's not I," said the dog.
"It's not I," said the frog.

"It's not I," said the hare.
"It's not I," said the bear.

"It is I," said the rain,
"Tapping at your windowpane."

A. G. Deming

RAINDROPS

Softly the rain goes pitter-patter,
Softly the rain comes falling down.
Hark to the people who hurry by;
Raindrops are footsteps from out the sky!
Softly the rain goes pitter-patter,
Softly the rain comes falling down.

THE RAIN

The rain came down in torrents
    And Mary said, "Oh, dear,
I'll have to wear my waterproof,
    And rubbers, too, I fear!"
So, carefully protected, she started off for school,
    When the big round sun
Came out and chuckled "April Fool!"

68

FIVE LITTLE CHICKENS

Said the first little chicken,
With a queer little squirm,
"Oh, I wish I could find
A fat little worm!"

Said the second little chicken,
With an odd little shrug,
"Oh, I wish I could find
A fat little bug!"

Said the third little chicken,
With a little sigh of grief,
"Oh, I wish I could find
A little green leaf!"

Said the fourth little chicken,
With a sharp little squeal,
"Oh, I wish I could find
Some nice yellow meal!"

Said the fifth little chicken,
With a faint little moan,
"I wish I could find
A wee gravel stone!"

"Now, see here," said their mother
From the green garden patch,
"If you want any breakfast,
You must all come and scratch!"

AROUND THE WORLD

In go-cart so tiny
    My sister I drew;
And I've promised to draw her
    The wide world through.

We have not yet started --
    I own it with sorrow --
Because our trip's always
    Put off till tomorrow.

Kate Greenaway

A BOY'S SONG

Where the pools are bright and deep,
Where the gray trout lies asleep,
Up the river, and over the lea,
That's the way for Billy and me.

Where the blackbird sings the latest,
Where the hawthorne blooms the sweetest,
Where the nestlings chirp and flee,
That's the way for Billy and me.

Where the mowers mow the cleanest,
Where the hay lies thick and greenest;
There to trace the homeward bee,
That's the way for Billy and me.

Where the hazel bank is steepest,
Where the shadow falls the deepest,
Where the clustering nuts fall free,
That's the way for Billy and me.

James Hogg

WHITE BUTTERFLIES

Fly, white butterflies, out to sea,
Frail, pale wings for the wind to try,
Small white wings that we scarce can see,
        Fly!

Some fly light as a laugh of glee,
Some fly soft as a long, low sigh;
All to the haven where each would be,
        Fly!

Algernon Charles Swinburne

MOTHER

Hundreds of stars in the deep blue sky,
    Hundreds of shells on the shore together,
Hundreds of birds that go singing by,
    Hundreds of birds in the sunny weather.

Hundreds of dewdrops to greet the dawn,
    Hundreds of bees in the purple clover,
Hundreds of butterflies on the lawn,
    But only one mother the wide world over.

George Cooper

TO MY VALENTINE

If apples were pears,
And peaches were plums,
And the rose had a different name —
If tigers were bears,
And fingers were thumbs,
I'd love you just the same!

BABY SEEDS

In a milkweed cradle,
    Snug and warm,
Baby seeds are hiding,
    Safe from harm.
Open wide the cradle,
    Hold it high!
Come, Mr. Wind,
    Help them fly.

GAELIC LULLABY

Hush! the waves are rolling in,
  White with foam, white with foam;
Father toils amid the din;
  But baby sleeps at home.

Hush! the winds roar hoarse and deep —
  On they come, on they come.
Brother seeks the wandering sheep;
  But baby sleeps at home.

Hush! the rain sweeps o'er the knolls,
  Where they roam, where they roam;
Sister goes to seek the cows;
  But baby sleeps at home.

ALL THROUGH THE NIGHT

Sleep, my babe, lie still and slumber,
All through the night,
Guardian angels God will lend thee,
All through the night;
Soft, the drowsy hours are creeping,
Hill and vale in slumber steeping,
Mother, dear, her watch is keeping,
All through the night.

GOOD NIGHT

Good night! Good night!
Far flies the light;
But still God's love
Shall flame above,
Making all bright.
Good night! Good night!

Victor Hugo

NOW I LAY ME DOWN

Now I lay me down to sleep,
I pray thee, Lord, my soul to keep;
Thy love go with me all the night,
And wake me with the morning light.

EARLY TO BED

Early to bed and early to rise
Makes a man healthy, wealthy and wise.

Old Proverb

73

MINNIE AND WINNIE

Minnie and Winnie
    Slept in a shell.
Sleep, little ladies!
    And they slept well.

Pink was the shell within,
    Silver without;
Sounds of the great sea
    Wandered about.

Sleep, little ladies!
    Wake not soon!
Echo on echo
    Dies to the moon.

Two bright stars
    Peeped into the shell.
"What are they dreaming of?
    Who can tell?"

Started a green linnet
    Out of the croft;
Wake, little ladies!
    The sun is aloft.

                    Alfred, Lord Tennyson

Index of First Lines